MW01235152

Gardener Growing and Harvesting Lettuce

Lettuce – Mainstay of the Salad Garden

Gardener's Guide to Growing Your Vegetable Garden Book IX

Paul R. Wonning

Gardeners' Guide Book Growing and Harvesting Lettuce

Published By Paul R. Wonning

Print Edition

paulwonning@gmail.com

If you would like email notification of when new Mossy Feet books become available email the author for inclusion in the subscription list.

Join Me on Facebook

Search Mossy Feet Books

Find them on www.mossyfeetbooks.com

Mossy Feet Books

Description

The *Gardeners' Guide Book Growing and Harvesting Lettuce* will provide needed information for the gardener to plant, grow and harvest this delectable crop in the vegetable salad garden. Lettuce culture is not hard allowing the knowledgeable gardener to grow several varieties for colorful, delicious salads.

Table of Contents

Gardeners' Guide Book Growing and Harvesting Lettuce
Paul R. Wonning

Introduction:

Easy to grow in the garden, lettuce provides tasty greens for salads and a top dressing for sandwiches and tacos. Grown as a spring or fall crop, lettuce can also over winter under a cold frame or unheated greenhouse, emerging in the spring to provide extra early greens from the garden.

Lettuce grows best during cool temperatures. Hot temperatures cause the plant to bolt to seed and the leaves to turn bitter. Plant breeders have developed hundreds of varieties and types of lettuce with many differing textures and flavors. The plant adapts well to a wide variety of soil and weather conditions.

Common Name:

Lettuce

The Roman name for lettuce was lactuca, meaning milk. The term referred to the milky sap that exuded from the cut ends of the plant The Roman name became laitues to the French. This name evolved into the English word Lettuce.

Botanical Name:

Lactuca sativa

The species name derives from the Latin name. The genus name, sativa, means "sown" or "cultivated" in Latin and differentiates the cultivated from the wild forms.

Family:

Compositae - Daisy

The Compositae family is on of the largest of the dicot families with over 25,000 species in about 1,620 genera. The name is used because of the flower type, which appears to be one flower but in reality is a composite of many flowers, called the florets, all sharing the same receptacle.

Light:

Lettuce needs full sun to light shade. Growing in the shade of other crops or under shading screen during the summer months can help prevent bolting. During the early spring and fall you can grow it in full sun.

Soil:

Lettuce requires well-drained soil. It is tolerant of a wide range of soils, but prefers well-drained, cool, loose soil with ample moisture. It likes a pH between 6.2 to 6.8. Lettuce is sensitive to low pH. Apply lime to achieve at least a ph of 6.0.

Hardiness Zone:

USDA Zones 4 – 9

Small plants are hardier than larger ones.

Origins and History:

Originally grown by the ancient Egyptians, people all over the world now enjoy its succulent leaves in salads, wraps and on sandwiches. The Egyptians first converted the wild plant to the edible plant we enjoy today. The use of lettuce spread from the Egyptians to the Greeks and Romans, who gave it its name.

Propagation:

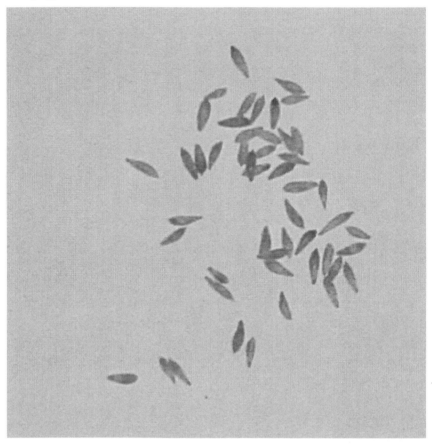

Propagate lettuce by planting seed.

Flower Time - Southern Indiana:

Lettuce will begin to bolt and flower after daytime temperatures begin to exceed seventy-five degrees and nighttime temperatures above sixty degrees. Another factor involves hours of daylight. When the lettuce has received a certain number of hours of daylight and the temperature warms, the plant will bolt to seed, causing the leaves to turn bitter. The bolting factors differ from cultivar to cultivar, but they are all similar. Once the plant starts to bolt, there is nothing to do but pull the plants. Unless you wish to save the seed, then leave the plant until the seed heads mature. The seeds have a cottony white fluff that develops when mature. Starting the seed under lights or in a cold frame or hot bed will give the plants a head start, allowing more time in the spring for the lettuce plants to develop. Using shade and row covers during the late spring or late summer for fall crops can help reduce bolting as well. Some varieties will resist bolting better than others will. The author has had success over wintering lettuce plants in an unheated cold frame to produce as many as two crops in the spring before bolting occurs.

Plant Height, Spread, Spacing:

Most lettuce varieties will grow to about six to twelve inches tall. Space lettuce plants about eight inches apart. The height and spread of lettuce will vary by variety, so it is best to use the seed packet as a guide. Flowering plants will get twenty-four to thirty six inches tall.

Flower Color, Description and Fragrance:

Lettuce flowers on stalks that can reach three feet tall. The lettuce is usually yellow in color, about an inch in diameter.

Plant Description:

Lettuce plants vary in height, depending upon cultivar, from six to twelve inches tall. The leaves vary in color, again depending upon cultivar, from green, red, burgundy, yellow and variations of two or more. Leaf texture also varies from smooth to crinkled, waxy and frilly. The root forms a taproot with a system of smaller roots surrounding it.

Planting Seeds:

Lettuce seed germinates the best between fifty to sixty five degrees but will germinate as low as forty degrees. Above eighty degrees, the seed can enter dormancy. At seventy degrees, the seed should germinate in a week, more or less. Plant the seed under lights or in a hot bed and cover with a light covering of fine peat moss. Keep the soil medium moist, but not soggy. Cover with clear plastic. Remove the cover after germination occurs. A common problem with lettuce seedlings is damping off. This is caused by too moist conditions and too little air circulation. Do not allow the soil medium to get soggy wet, though it must be kept moist. Gardeners can direct seed lettuce seeds by late winter for early spring. Germination will vary due to temperature conditions. Use spacing recommendations on the seed packet as variety requirement varies. Plant lettuce seeds in rows or beds, covering the seed about 1/8 inch of fine soil. Broadcasting the seed in beds instead of planting in rows works well. The seeds do need light to germinate, so do not cover with too much soil.

Growing Seedlings:

Transplant the young seedlings when the first true leaves appear, usually about a week to ten days after the initial seed leaves emerge. Transplant to individual pots and move to a cold frame or greenhouse.

An unheated greenhouse will do fine, as the seedlings can stand some freezing temperatures. Keep well watered, but not soggy. Transplant when the roots have filled the pot. Since lettuce can stand cold weather, it is safe to transplant them a few weeks before the last spring frost. If fall planting, the plants will stand temperatures down to about twenty-eight degrees Fahrenheit with little or no damage. Covering them with a spun bond row cover will also help them.

Garden Culture and Uses:

It is best to improve the soil the fall before planting by incorporating compost or rotted manure. It is best to plant a number of different varieties with varying maturity dates. This will ensure a longer harvest than less reliable ones as changing weather conditions can cause one verities to bolt while another matures. Keep the soil moist because the shallow root system does not allow the plant to delve too deeply for water. Shade the plants in the summer to reduce the sunlight and heat. This can help reduce bolting. Moisture stress and high temperatures can encourage bolting. Plant fall crops timed to mature around the time of the first fall frosts. Use row covers, spun bond to protect against frost. Mature plants are not as frost tolerant as seedlings but can still stand subfreezing temperature with a little protection.

Problems:

The author has encountered few problems with lettuce over the years. The only two on this short list that have ever appeared were slugs and aphids, never in any quantity to bother treating.

Foliage Rot

This usually occurs during periods of extreme rainfall. The leaves turn brown and rot. The best cure is to try to provide adequate drainage to the soil and ventilation to the air around the plants.

Aphids

Aphids are small insects that are about the size of a dressmaker's pinhead, or smaller. They suck juices from plant stems and leaves, weakening them. The insects can be green, orange, red, yellow or white and are wingless. Ants sometimes sustain colonies of them so they can feed on the honeydew the insects secrete. These pests can multiply quickly, so if you notice them, it is best to eradicate quickly. Small infestations can be "wiped" off with a finger or crushed between finger and thumb. Use horticultural oil, insecticidal soap or a solution of Ivory soap. Do not use detergent, as detergents can harm plants. Use a homemade solution of one teaspoon of Ivory soap and a pinch of cayenne pepper to one quart of water. Spray on afflicted plants. Ladybugs feed on aphids in large quantities. Purchasing ladybugs and releasing is a gamble. Most of the insects will likely fly off.

Earwigs

Earwigs are about one inch long and are dark brown to black. They have a set of forceps on their back end that makes identification easy. These bugs are party beneficial, as they will feed on aphids and other annoying insects. But they enjoy munching on celery, lettuce and other garden goodies. They enjoy dark places where they will hide during the day. There are insecticides to kill them, but first you can try using traps. Simply lay small boards around the garden. The earwigs should hide under them. Lift the boards in the morning and catch them, dumping them into soapy water to kill them.

White Mold

White mold is a fungal disease that affects many plants. White mold appears as a whitish, cottony looking growth that occurs on lesions that form on afflicted plants. The plants may wilt and die. Get rid of infected plants and do not compost them. That can spread the disease. Use approved fungicides to treat and try not to let the garden area get soaking wet for long periods of time as that encourages fungal growth. Once it is in the soil, it will stay active for years. Sometimes using plastic mulch will prevent exposure by preventing contact with the ground. If feasible, remove the soil and discard it, replacing it with new soil. Or move the garden; if possible, making sure you do not infect the new site with soiled shoes, tools, etc.

Slugs

These are sort of like snails without shells. They can be troublesome, but are seldom a major problem. Use diatomaceous earth to dust around the garden soil and on the plants. There are some commercially available traps and baits that will work. A small quantity of salt sprinkled on them will kill them. Do not use a lot of salt, as it can affect your garden soil.

Medicinal uses:

Because of its dietary fiber content, lettuce can act as a mild laxative. It also contains a mild sedative, so it can help with insomnia. The bulky leaves can aid in weight loss when consumed before a meal, as they will fill the stomach, causing it to feel full. Consuming before a meal can also aid digestion, as can help tone the stomach. Its low carbohydrate content makes it an ideal food for diabetics.

Food Uses:

Lettuce is usually consumed raw as a green in salads or as a garnish for sandwiches. Combined with other vegetables, like carrots, onion and radishes lettuce makes a tasty salad. Lettuce is also the primary ingredient in lettuce soup.

Harvesting:

Harvest lettuce anytime the leaves have reached a usable size. One strategy is to plant the seeds close together, then instead of thinning, cut every other plant to eat while young. The remaining plants will have more room then to grow. If you notice the plants begin to elongate, harvest and store in the refrigerator. Cut the lettuce with a sharp knife slightly above ground level, if possilbe. The lettuce should keep many days if stored properly. Many times the plants will resprout after harvest, leading to a second harvest.

Storage:

After harvest, wash the lettuce with cold water. Allow to drip dry or in a salad spinner. Store the lettuce in a plastic bag that will maintain high humidity in the crisper drawer of the refrigerator. It stores best at or slightly above freezing temperatures. Fresh-cut lettuce should store well for a week or more.

Groups:

Green Leaf

Red Leaf

The leaf lettuces are the most widely grown of the lettuces. The plants form crisp leaves along a central stalk. many of these may send up new shoots when harvested.

Cos or Romaine

Romain lettuces form an elongated head that can stand longer in the garden than other types.

Butterhead

Butterheads form small, loose heads. The leaves have a sweet, delicate flavor.

Heading or Crisphead

these form large, crips heads. These types are the touchiest and will bolt sooner than other types. They need a long, cool growing season to mature properly. Fall crops may have a better chance of maturing withhout bolting.

Stem or Asparagus

Stem lettuces form a large seedstalk that cooks use in soups, creamed or in Chinese dishes.

Nutrition:

Nutrition Facts (One cup raw leaf lettuce, chopped)

Calories 9

Dietary Fiber 1.3

Protein 1 gram

Carbohydrates 1.34 grams

Vitamin A 1456 IU

Vitamin C 13.44

Calcium 20.16

Iron 0.62

Potassium 162.4 mg

Cultivars:

Gardeners will find hundreds of varieties of lettuce on the market. This is not an all inclusive list, but includes most of the varieties found in seed catalog selections.

Butterhead Lettuce

Matina Sweet Lettuce

55-65 days

A compact butterhead that has outstanding flavor and attractive appearance. Matina Sweet is very heat tolerant.

Winter Brown Lettuce

50-55 days

This green with reddish brown overlay lettuce forms a smaller size loose head.

Tom Thumb Lettuce

34 days

This unusual miniature butterhead lettuce produces heads about the size of a baseball.

Drunken Woman Frizzy Headed Lettuce

55 days

While we won't even venture to hypothesize where the "drunken woman" part of the name comes from, the "frizzled" leaves.

Continuity Lettuce

56 days, 75 days fall sown

This popular variety is one of the most widely grown lettuce.

Buttercrunch Lettuce

48 days

Buttercrunch is similar to bib types but with thick, juicy green leaves and a small tight head.

Arctic King Lettuce

150 days

This butterhead is able to withstand the most severe maritime winters with only minimal cover.

Deliane Lettuce

48-50 days

You'll fall in love with Deliane, as it's a simply irresistible butterhead.

Avicenna Lettuce

45-50 days

This eye-catching, ruby-colored, butterhead sports smooth, thick, crunchy leaves.

Crisphead Lettuce

Red Iceberg Lettuce

50 days

A colorful alternative to the rather ordinary green iceberg types.

Mini Green Lettuce

55-60 days

This pocket-sized iceberg is an irresistible curiosity, fun to grow and eat.

Superior 1 Lettuce Organic

60 days

Proving its superior performance in our lettuce trials, this organic selection is true to its name.

Joker Lettuce Organic

50-60 days

This crisphead produces dense, 6-8 inch heads.

Optima Lettuce

54 days

One of the darkest green Boston lettuces on the market.

Victoria Lettuce Organic

45 days

A rich green butterhead type that forms an amazingly heavy, upright, open, ten inch diameter head.

Speckles Lettuce

50 days

Speckles is an old American variety with red and green variegated leaves and dark speckles.

Flashy Butter Oak Lettuce

54 days

Exquisite melding of shape, color, taste, texture and form. Compact plants.

North Pole Lettuce

50 days

This is one outstanding cold weather performer. North Pole is a sweet, compact, light green butterhead.

Carmona Lettuce

54 days

A truly transcendent butterhead. Its shapely plants have dense, pale, yellow-green hearts wrapped loosely.

Mafalda Lettuce Organic

LT462

55-60 days

Butterhead with big, classic form, light green, smooth, supple leaves.

French Crisp/Batavia Lettuce

Loma Lettuce

48 days

This French Crisp variety boasts glossy, dark green leaves.

Mottistone Lettuce

55 days

Batavia types are sometimes referred to as 'summercrisp' lettuces for their densely packed hearts and ability to resist summer heat.

Loose-Leaf Lettuce

Two Star Lettuce

45 days

Revolution Lettuce

38 days

Frilly leaved lollo rossa type lettuce with a deep, intense red color.

Simpson Elite Lettuce

53 days

Extremely slow bolting, Simpson Elite produces attractive, neon green, loose heads with broad, crumpled, curled leaves.

Red Sails Lettuce

53 days

Up to 10 inches across, the crinkled and deeply fringed leaves are burgundy-turning to medium green at the base.

Salad Bowl Lettuce

50 days

Pom Pom Lettuce

46 days

Each plant is a small, beautiful rounded mass of densely packed, with a green pom pom shape.

Green Ice Lettuce Organic

50 days

multi-harvest, loose-leaf lettuce. Uniform plants have delightfully wavy margins and bright green leaves.

New Red Fire Lettuce

29 days

Ruby-red loose-leaf variety.

Oaky Red Splash Lettuce

48 days

Oak leaf lettuce with green tinged leaves.

Green Deer Tongue Lettuce

50 days

A distinctive lettuce that looks much like a seven to eight inch pinwheel growing in the garden. Olive green leaves.

Sunset Lettuce

52 days

This is a vivid red, puckered-leaf lettuce.

Italienischer Lettuce

55 days

Cantarix Lettuce

50-55 days

Cantarix produces beautiful billowing globes of glossy, maroon-colored, oak leaf foliage.

Merlot Lettuce

55 days

Striking, deep dark red, almost purple frilly leaves.

Mascara Lettuce

48 days

A very uniform, dark red oak leaf type.

Encino Lettuce

50-55 days

lettuce produces enormous plants

Relic Lettuce

60 days

A handsome lettuce that's a real standout.

Galiano Lettuce

50 days

First-rate flavor, appearance, uniformity, and field-holding ability.

Marin Lettuce

55-60 days

Marin's emerald green leaves are wildly wavy and an attractive green.

Romaine Lettuce

Eiffel Tower Lettuce

65 days

This refined romaine has an unusually tall and cylindrical shape that's picturesque in the garden.

Winter Density Lettuce

65 days

 An early, short romaine type with a very good upright growth habit. It reaches a height of 8 inches.

Valmaine Lettuce

56 days

A flavorful romaine with very thick and meaty, emerald green leaves.

Little Gem Lettuce

33 days

Devils Tongue Lettuce

55 days

This unique romaine has a dramatic red coloration befitting its rich flavor.

Flashy Trout's Back Lettuce

55 days

Outredgeous Lettuce

52 days. Outredgeous is a wonderful, stout-growing variety that can be harvested either as a baby lettuce or allowed to mature to a nice head.

Bullet Lettuce

50 days

Bullet is a healthy, vigorously growing romaine that is very sweet, crunchy, and succulent.

Crisp Mint Lettuce

60-65 days

Olga Lettuce

65 days

Marshall Lettuce

65 days

Marshall is a deep red romaine.

Dazzle Lettuce

35 days

A ruby-red Little Gem-type lettuce. A palm-sized, mini romaine with succulent leaves.

Spretnak Lettuce

45-55 days

Tantan Lettuce

50-55 days

Truchas Lettuce

45-55 days

Strikingly red, small statured romaine type.

Coastal Star Lettuce

57 days

A stately, tall romaine with heavy, deep green heads that reach ten inches high and 7 inches wide.

Breen Lettuce

50 days

A perfectly-formed, petite, red romaine.

Cooking and Preparing:

Most people consume lettuce raw in salads or as a tasty addition to sandwiches. Many people make lettuce soup from pureed lettuce, onion, potato and chicken stock. Chinese cooks stir fry lettuce and some cooks like to grill it. Romaine lettuce is especially good for grilling. To grill, remove the outter leaves, split in half and sprinkle with olive oil and salt. Grill until lightly charred and serve with a dressing made with equal parts sour cream and blue chees

Seed Companies to Buy Lettuce Seed:

Burpee

W. Atlee Burpee Company

Warminster PA 18974

1-800-888-1447

The W. Atlee Burpee Company is one of the leading seed companies

in the gardening industry. The catalog lists good selections of annual and

perennial flowers as well as vegetable seeds. Many, many tomatoes listed in

addition to sweet corn and squash.

http://www.burpee.com/

Farmers Seed and Nursery

Division of Plantron, Inc

818 NW 4th Street

Fairbault, MN 55021

1-850-7334-1623

This catalog has a good selection of nursery stock including ornamental shrubs and trees. Fruit includes strawberries, blackberries and raspberries. Other types of fruit trees and vines, too. Nut trees, perennial plants and roses, also. There is a good selection of vegetable seed.

http://www.farmerseed.com/

George W. Park Seed Company

1 Parkton Ave

Greenwood, SC 29647-0001

1-800-845-3369

This bountiful catalog has extensive offerings of all categories of seeds - herbs, vegetables, annual and perennial seeds. There is also a generous offering of fruit and berry plants like grapes, blackberries and strawberries.

http://www.parkseed.com/

Gurney's Seed and Nursery

PO Box 4178

Greendale, IN 47025-4178

513-354-1491

Gurney's large format catalog offers large selections of vegetables, flowers, fruits and supplies for gardening. They also list trees, shrubs, roses, and nut trees. This is one of the older seed companies, they have been selling seeds for many years.

http://www.gurneys.com/

Harris Seeds

355 Paul Road

PO Box 24966

Rochester, NY 14624-0966

1-800-514-4441

Heavy selection of vegetable seeds, with a nice offering of flower seeds, too. They have almost 20 pages of gardening supplies like seed starting equipment, flats and carts.

http://www.harrisseeds.com/

John Scheepers Kitchen Garden Seeds

23 Tulip Drive

PO Box 838

Bantam, CT 06750-0638

1-860-567-6086

www.kitchengardenseeds.com

This catalog focuses on vegetables and herbs. It has unusual and old time varieties as well as some of the favorites. The salad green selection of seeds is excellent. There are also Asian greens and sprouting seeds. There are some flower seeds, mostly annual fragrant and cutting flowers. This is a nice catalog with some unusual seed offerings.

Johnny's Selected Seeds

955 Benton Ave.

Winslow, ME 04901

Phone: 877-564-6697

Fax: 800-738-6314

Annuals

Bulbs

Perennials

Flower, Vegetable and Wildflower Seeds

Fruit Trees and Berries

Garden Supplies, Tools and Power Equipment

Gifts and Decorative Accessories

Greenhouses and Indoor Gardening Supplies

Ground Covers, Shrubs, Trees, and Vines

Herbs and Vegetables

Irrigation Supplies and Equipment

Fertilizer, Weed & Pest Control Products

Magazines and Books

Ornamental Grasses and Plants

Johnny's Selected Seeds is a mail-order seed producer and merchant located in Albion and Winslow, Maine, USA. The company was established in 1973 by our Founder and Chairman Rob Johnston, Jr. Johnny's prides itself on its superior product, research, technical information, and service for home gardeners and commercial growers.

Our products include vegetable seeds, medicinal and culinary herb seeds, and flower seeds. We also offer unique, high quality gardening tools and supplies. Our Export Department ships seeds internationally, and welcomes your inquiry. Of course, we also ship throughout the United States. We sell both retail and wholesale, small to large quantities.

Website: Johnnyseeds.com

Email Contact: homegarden@johnnyseeds.com

J. W. Jung Seed Company

335 South High Street

Randolph, WI 53957-0001

1-800-247-5864

http://www.jungseed.com/

Jung sells a very interesting mix of fruit trees and plants, shrubs and

trees, vegetable and flower seed, and gardening supplies. Perennial plants,

flower bulbs, lilies and roses are included in the offerings. This is a

"must have" catalog for the gardener.

Pinetree Garden Seeds

PO Box 300

New Gloucester, ME 04260

1-926-3400

http://www.superseeds.com/

The catalog claims over 900 varieties of seeds, bulbs, tubers, garden books and products. The listings are pretty extensive with the emphasis on vegetable seeds. There are sections for ethnic vegetables like Asian, Italian, and Latin American. The flower offerings include both annual and perennial flower seeds. The garden book section is impressive, boasting 14 pages of gardening related books. Several pages of garden supplies, there is

even a Garden-opoly game.

Seeds of Change

PO Box 15700

Santa Fe NM 87592-1500

1-888-762-7333

http://www.seedsofchange.com/

This catalog is for vegetable lovers as it is mostly devoted to them, and all seeds sold by this company are certified organic. There is a section of flower seeds, but veggies take center stage. There is a full

page of garlic varieties! Gourmet greens and herbs are in good supply, too.

There is also a good selection of gardening books and gardening supplies.

Select Seeds

180 Stickney Hill Road

Union, CT 06076

1-860-684-9310

http://www.selectseeds.com/

If you are looking for something a bit out of the mainstream or "different" then Select Seeds is the catalog you are looking for. Most of the seeds and plants offered are not found in the major outlets. Special sections for fragrant and old fashioned plants are featured. This catalog is a must for the home gardener looking for a flower garden that stands out a bit.

Seymours Selected Seeds

334 West Stroud Street

Randolph, WI 53596

1-800-353-9516

http://www.seymourseedusa.com/

This small catalog is packed with a full selection of annual and

perennial flowers for the home gardner. Many unusual varieties and

old time favorites. There is also a nice selection of bulbs and perennial

plants.

Southern Exposure Seed Exchange

PO Box 460

Mineral, VA 23117

Phone: 540-894-9480

Fax: 540-894-9481

http://www.southernexposure.com/

Annuals

Bulbs

Perennials

Exotic Plants and Flowers

Flower, Vegetable and Wildflower Seeds

Fruit Trees and Berries

Garden Supplies, Tools and Power Equipment

Gifts and Decorative Accessories

Ground Covers, Shrubs, Trees, and Vines

Herbs and Vegetables

Irrigation Supplies and Equipment

Fertilizer, Weed & Pest Control Products

Magazines and Books

Ornamental Grasses and Plants

Other

We are a wonderful source for vegetables selected in a day where taste and local adaptability were the primary factors. We have an extensive line of heirloom and other open pollinated seeds and seed saving supplies. Many of our varieties are certified organic. We also carry a wide variety of garlic and perennial onion bulbs and medicinal herb rootstock. We are a source for naturally colored cotton seeds. Many of our products are Certified Organic.

Website: www.southernexposure.com

Email Contact: gardens@southernexposure.com

Swallowtail Garden Seeds

122 Calistoga Road, #178

Santa Rosa, CA 95409

Phone: Toll Free 1-877-489-7333

707-538-3585

http://www.swallowtailgardenseeds.com/

Territorial Seed Company

PO Box 158

Cottate Grove, OR 97424

1-541-942-9547

http://www.territorialseed.com/

This is a good catalog for market gardeners. Territoral has a big selection of vegetables. There are a lot of different varieties of beans, with 25 pound bags available many varieties. Sweet and popcorn also well represented. Many varieties of lettuce also listed. Melons, peppers, peas, pumpkins and squash, along with boatloads of tomatoes. They also have a large selecion of annual flowers, available in larger quantities, so small greenhouse growers would find this catalog helpful. There are approximately 30 varieties of sunflowers, and lots of herbs. There is a good selection of growing supplies, including several types of spun bond fabric row covers. You will find a pretty good selection of organic growing aids in here also.Also a small selection of honey bee supplies, including a mason bee starter kit.

Thompson and Morgan

220 Faraday Ave

Jackson NJ 08527

1-800-274-7333

http://www.thompsonandmorgan.com/

200 pages of pure joy! Thompson and Morgan is one of the most complete seed catalogs available to the home gardener. You will find something of everything including the most popular annual and perennial flowers, vegetables and herbs, tree seeds and houseplants. There are hard to find varieties,

standard varieties and some downright odd and unusual varieties.

This catalog focuses on seeds, so you won't find many gardening supplies.

Thompson and Morgan is one seed catalog the serious gardener shouldn't be

without.

Totally Tomatoes

334 West Stroud Street

Randolph, WI 53956

1-800-345-5977

http://www.totallytomato.com/

41 pages of nothing but tomatoes. They have the standard varieties available everywhere like Burpee Big Boy and Park Whopper. But there are many hard to find varieties like Aunt Ruby's German Green, Dixie Golden Giant and Bloody Butcher. They also have a good selection of peppers (16 pages), salad greens and cucumbers. Nice catalog and very interesting.

Urban Farmer Seeds

4105 Indiana 32 West

Westfield, IN 46074

1-317-600-2807

customerservice@ufseeds.com

http://www.ufseeds.com/

Vermont Bean Seed Company

334 W Stroud Street

Randolph, WI 53956

800-349-1071

http://www.vermontbean.com/

These folks really do have the beans, sixteen pages of them. The catalog is chuck full of other stuff, too. Vegetable seeds are in good supply as well as some flower seeds and herbs. They also sell vegetable and flower plants.

Garden supplies include a nice selection of organic garden aids,and seed starting supplies.

Acknowledgements

https://en.wikipedia.org/wiki/Lettuce

https://extension.illinois.edu/veggies/lettuce.cfm

http://www.gardening.cornell.edu/homegardenin
g/scene9aa6.html

https://bonnieplants.com/growing/growing-
lettuce/

http://www.almanac.com/plant/lettuce

About the Author

Gardening, history and travel seem an odd soup in which to stew one's life, but Paul has done just that. A gardener since 1975, he has spent his spare time reading history and traveling with his wife. He gardens, plans his travels and writes his books out in the sticks near a small town in southeast Indiana. He enjoys sharing the things he has learned about gardening, history and travel with his readers. The many books Paul has written reflect that joy of sharing. He also writes fiction in his spare time. Read and enjoy his books, if you will. Or dare.

Now, back to writing, if he can get the cat off the keyboard.

Join Paul on Facebook

https://www.facebook.com/Mossy-Feet-Books-474924602565571/

Twitter

https://twitter.com/MossyFeetBooks

mossyfeetbooks@gmail.com

Mossy Feet Books Catalog

To Get Your Free Copy of the Mossy Feet Books Catalogue, Click This Link.

http://mossyfeetbooks.blogspot.com/

Gardening Books

Fantasy Books

Humor

Science Fiction

Semi – Autobiographical Books

Travel Books

Gardener's Guide to Gardening Tools

Paul R. Wonning

Garden Trowels

A garden trowel is an indispensable tool for every gardener. All gardeners should have one trowel and it is best to have several for different purposes. The word trowel derives from the Latin word "truella", which means "small ladle". A trowel can serve as a ladle but that is really just one use for a trowel. Indeed, a trowel is the most used tool in the gardener's toolbox so it is important to get a good one. Nothing is as aggravating as a poor quality trowel that bends when you try to dig. Additionally, a poorly designed handle tires the hand and causes blisters.

There is an incredible variety of hand trowels available to the modern gardener. The gardener will find wood handle trowels and plastic composite trowels. Also available are aluminum and stainless steel trowels. New ergonomic designs make gardening easier on the hands. They also make it more accessible to those with repetitive stress injury and arthritis. These new designs include gel filled handles and curved designs that are more natural for the hand to hold while using them.

Finding a good garden hand trowel from this vast selection of trowels is a bit confusing. So take your time and then choose the garden hand trowel best suited for your needs.

Ergonomic Trowels

Ergonomic trowels use a new design to provide ergonomic ease of use. Some of the new ergonomic trowels help gardeners with arthritis continue their garden activities. These tools also help gardeners without those disorders to garden with less stress to their hands and wrists.

The ergonomic design of the trowel's handle allows the gardener to use a more natural position while working. A cushioned grip helps prevent blisters. These trowels are usually composed of an alloy consisting of cast aluminum and magnesium so they are light and strong. The blade's design allows you to punch into the soil easily and lift a manageable load of soil. The curved shapes provide a more balanced transfer of energy from the hand and wrist to the trowel. This reduces hand fatigue common when using a hand garden trowel.

Gel Ergonomic Trowels

Gel ergonomic trowels provide a cushioned grip that prevent blisters and make working in the garden more fun. Gardeners abuse their hands a lot with all that digging, pruning and chopping. Any tool which helps reduce that abuse is a welcome addition to any gardener's tool chest. A gel grip trowel helps your hands by incorporating a cushioned, gel filled handle into the garden trowel's design.

This gel flexes and provides cushioning to hard-working fingers while digging. Some of these feature a serrated edge to open bags of fertilizer or other gardening material and to cut roots while digging. Others have stainless steel blades.

Stainless Steel Trowels

Stainless steel is an ideal component to use to make trowels. It is strong, durable and resists rust. They also polish to a high sheen so they are attractive as well. The shiny metal is easy to spot if the gardener misplaced the tool while pursuing other projects in the garden. Stainless steel trowels usually have wood handles. These trowels are prone to rusting over time.

Nursery Trowels

The small, lightweight nursery trowel works well in tight spaces. The long handle of the nursery trowel allows you to reach into tight spots and the small, light blade makes it an ideal trowel for women to use.

Soil Scoop Trowels

A soil scoop is a specialized trowel that will certainly find many uses in and around the garden. The scoop is great for those who mix their own potting soil, as it will allow you to scoop vermiculate, peat moss and other soil components. The scoop will also work great to pot up plants and fill bedding packs for small transplants. Using the scoop, you can pick up potting soil from the bag or bin and place it where you want it. This help to fill in around roots under and around stems and leaves.

A soil scoop will work better than a trowel to fill in soil around newly transplanted shrubs and flowers in the garden. It can also scoop fertilizer and other bulk garden products into spreaders. Specialized bonsai soil scoops work great to fill soil in and around the small pots used in bonsai. Their unique shape fits in under the leaves and branches of these miniature trees better than a trowel. The right soil scoop fills a void left by the hand trowel. Standard trowels are great for digging and weeding. However, their shape is usually not suitable for scooping soil for potting and bonsai needs.

Aluminum Trowel

Aluminum trowels are strong, durable and lightweight. Aluminum resists corrosion, so if you accidentally leave your trowel out in the rain it will not rust. Since aluminum trowels are cast in one piece, the blade will not separate from the handle, as it will with some other types of trowels. Aluminum is a soft metal and it will not hold a sharp edge as a steel trowel will. Since it is not a strong as steel, aluminum garden trowels may bend easier if you are digging in heavy soil. The blades of an aluminum trowel may also chip if you strike a rock while digging. Aluminum trowels usually have a plastic grip on the handle to cushion your hand. Rubberized grips are easier on the hand than the polypropylene ones.

Wood Handle Trowels

The traditional handle for a garden trowel has been wood. Wood, usually a hardwood like ash or hickory, is the traditional choice for a handle for a trowel. Attractive, strong and durable many manufacturers still make trowels with wood handles. However, it tends to split, especially if you accidentally leave the trowel out in the weather.

Trowel Maintenance

Protect the trowel from rust with a coating of old motor oil or cooking oil when not in use. A good spray with aerosol cooking oil before using will make the trowel easier to clean when finished with it. Alternatively, fill a bucket with sand and saturate it with oil. Use this to dip your hand tools in to clean them and add a protective sheen of oil to help prevent rust. Sometimes it is helpful to file or grind the edges of steel trowels to a sharp edge to make it easier to cut into soil. Paint the handles or blades a bright orange or yellow to make them more visible. This makes it less likely to lose the trowel or leave it out in the weather.

The wide variety of trowels on the market can intimidate even the most seasoned gardener. Trowels come in different shapes, sizes, materials and colors. Picking the right type of trowel is easier if the gardener is aware of the many different types available and the uses of each.

Gardeners' Guide to Botany

Formation and Structure of the Seed in Angiosperms

This article deals strictly with seed formation in the class of plants called angiosperms, or "enclosed seeds." It also deals with the further division of the dicots, or plants with two seed leaves.

The seed is the structure which develops from the fertilized ovule of the flower. The seed comprises all of the genetic information required to produce a new plant like the plant from which it originated. It is composed of three distinct structures, the embryo, the endosperm and the seed coat. The formation of these structures occurs during the process called fertilization. Fertilization occurs, as it does with all flowering plants, after a grain of pollen, produced by the anther of a flower, lands on the stigma of a flower of the same species. When this occurs the pollen grains grow a tube which extends down through the style into the ovary. The sperm cells from the pollen travel down the tube and then fuse with the nuclei of an egg cell that is within the ovary.

In angiosperms double fertilization occurs during this process. One fertilization method involves the fusion of sperm cell nuclei with an egg cell. This part of the fertilization forms the zygote which develops into a pro zygote and then into the embryo. A secondary fertilization involves second sperm cell nuclei and the polar nuclei. This fertilization forms the endosperm.

This double fertilization has formed two of the three parts of the seed, the embryo and the endosperm. The seed coat develops over the endosperm and the embryo, protecting them from the elements and holding the parts together.

A zygote is the cell, which forms after sexual fertilization, occurs. This zygote contained within the seed is the undeveloped plant and within it is all the genetic information needed for the plant to grow. This genetic information, or DNA, comes from both parent plants which contributed to the initial fertilization. If self fertilization has occurred, which happens in many types of plants, the genetic material comes from a single plant. After formation of the seed the zygote develops into a pro zygote which then develops into the embryo. The embryo becomes inactive, waiting for conditions to become satisfactory for germination. Depending upon the plant species and storage conditions a zygote can remain in this inactive state for a period of hours to many, many years after the seed forms. Some plant seeds will germinate immediately after they fall from the plant. Other plant seeds will need a complicated series of developments to trigger germination. The zygote consists of two portions, one of which will form the stem and leaves. The other portion will form the root of the plant. In dicot plants there are two seed leaves present which will emerge upon germination and produce food for the plant until the true leaves develop.

The endosperm is quick to develop after fertilization. Once the endosperm develops it too will remain inactive until after germination occurs. The purpose of the endosperm in the seed structure is to serve as a food source for the embryo to use once germination begins. The embryo will draw upon this food source until the roots and the leaves develop well enough to draw nutrients from the soil and gather light from the sun and manufacture the food the plant needs to survive.

The seed coat's purpose in the structure of the seed is to protect the embryo and endosperm. Seed coats develop from the ovule of the flower and it will remain in place until germination occurs. The seed coat sheds off at this point. Once the seed forms it enters a state of dormancy. Dormancy can last for hours, days, weeks or years, depending upon the species of the plants and its growth requirements.

Mossy Feet Books
www.mossyfeetbooks.com

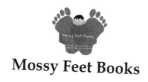

Mossy Feet Books

Made in the USA
Columbia, SC
11 July 2024

38492449R00028